The F-4 in the Air National Guard

PHANTOM GUARDIANS

The F-4 in the Air National Guard

PHANTOM GUARDIANS

Daniel Soulaine

OSPREY
AEROSPACE

Published in 1992 by Osprey Publishing Limited
59 Grosvenor Street, London W1X 9DA

© Daniel Soulaine

ISBN 1 85532 198 X

Editor Dennis Baldry
Page design Paul Kime
Printed in Hong Kong

Front cover A May 1990 study of
two RF-4C Phantom IIs assigned to
the 106th Tactical Reconnaissance
Squadron, Alabama Air National
Guard (*Don Spering/AIR*)

Back cover A quartet of RF-4Cs
from the 106th TRS salute the USS
Alabama Memorial, near Mobile (*Don
Spering/AIR*)

Title page Rolling back the years, an
F-4C from the 136th Fighter
Interceptor Squadron, New York
ANG, heads for the heavens. On 5
November 1966, 63-7541 destroyed
a North Vietnamese MiG-21 in the
war-torn skies of Southeast Asia (*Don
Spering/AIR*)

Right Hot pursuit: intent on
intercepting a fellow 136th FIS
Phantom that launched from Niagara
Falls International Airport ten
minutes earlier, this pair of F-4Cs stay
in afterburner as the gears travel into
the wells. The aircraft are armed with
inert AIM-9 Sidewinders

For a catalogue of all books published by Osprey Aerospace
please write to:

**The Marketing Department,
Octopus Illustrated Books, 1st Floor, Michelin House,
81 Fulham Road, London SW3 6RB**

Introduction

Phantom! Designed for the US Navy as a carrier-borne interceptor, the McDonnell F-4B Phanton II became operational with the Fleet in 1962. Subsequently adopted by the US Air Force as its prime tactical fighter, the Phantom became the most outstanding multi-role combat aircraft in the western world.

The largest operator by far, the US Air Force took delivery of over 2700 Phantoms between 1962 and 1974. In the early seventies, the Air Force began to transfer the first of many Phantoms to the Air National Guard, with no less than 29 units being equipped with the F-4C, F-4D, F-4E and RF-4C. When these words were written in October 1991, almost all of the fighter versions had been retired in favour of the F-15 and F-16, but some RF-4C units are scheduled to survive beyond the year 2000.

This book is intended to be a retrospective of the many camouflage schemes and unit markings carried by ANG Phantoms. Four official paint schemes – Southeast Asia, wrap-around, Europe One and low-visibility grey – have been applied to ANG Phantoms. Many units designed imaginative squadron markings, while others were content to comply with the technical orders. The 'one-off' paint schemes and markings used for operational evaluations or to celebrate special occasions, are also included on the following pages.

This Aerospace Colour Series volume would not have been possible without the help given by ANG units and their enthusiastic personnel, and by many 'fellow travellers'. I especially want to thank Craig Baldwin, Bryan Beaton, Peter Becker, David F Brown, Regent Dansereau, René J Francillon, Major Larry Harrington/North Dakota ANG, Tom Hildreth, Harold Homuth, Mike Kopack, Duncan MacIntosh, Patrick Martin, Ruud van Nimwegen, Robert Pfannenschmidt, Yves Richard, Douglas E Slowiak/Vortex Photo Graphics, Keith Snyder and Don Spering/AIR. Finally, I should like to thank my wife Suzanne for her tremendous moral support.

Right Carrying an asymmetric load of a 600 US gal centreline tank and a 370 US gal wing tank, a sharkmouthed F-4E of the 110th TFS, Missouri ANG, taxies out for take-off at Lambert Field, St Louis

Contents

Alabama 106th TRS

In February 1971, the 106th Tactical Reconnaissance Squadron had the distinction of being the first Air National Guard unit to receive the McDonnell Douglas F-4 Phantom II. Based at Birmingham Municipal Airport, the squadron is still operating the reconnaissance version of the F-4, and has no replacement in sight.

The 106th TRS flew the Republic RF-84F Thunderflash for fourteen years before transitioning to the RF-4C Phantom II. During their early years with the squadron, the RF-4Cs were painted in standard SE Asia camouflage and markings (RF-4C 64-1038; *LB Slides*)

In order to enhance pilot-proficiency, the 106th TRS operated this single F-4C
for a limited period. Taken in September 1981, this shot confirms that the
aircraft was painted in the same squadron markings as applied to the RF-4C
(F-4C 63-7468; *Don Spering/AIR*)

The 106th TRS repainted its fleet in the Europe One camouflage scheme during the early eighties. While the unit markings remained minimal, the top of the vertical stabilizer was either painted yellow, green, blue or red to denote each flight (RF-4C 64-1032)

Above The 106th TRS adopted the BH tailcode, for Birmingham, when it repainted its Phantoms in the low viz grey scheme. This aircraft was participating in RAM '88 (Reconnaissance Air Meet 1988), at Bergstrom AFB, Texas when this shot was taken in August 1988 (RF-4C 65-893; *Daniel Soulaine Collection*)

Right Close up of the tail marking specially applied to the three Phantoms that participated in RAM '88 (RF-4C 64-1044; *Keith Snyder*)

Above Photographed at McConnell AFB, Texas in April 1990, the wing commander's RF-4C is decorated with a highlighted tailcode and wing designation, full colour ANG badge and a special marking on the jet intake. The groundcrew even made customized covers for the camera ports in the nose (RF-4C 65-854)

Right The RF-4Cs assigned to the squadron and wing commanders of the Alabama ANG fly fast and low during a tactical reconnaissance exercise. Also featured on the front cover, both aircraft have highlighted tail 'feathers'; the leading Phantom (the wing commander's aircraft), features the special marking on the jet intake (RF-4C, 65-854/65-843; *Don Spering/AIR*)

The unique marking applied to 65-854 represents the various units (squadrons and groups/wings) around the 117th TFW badge, with the famous 'Spook' Phantom mascot above it

Missouri 110th TFS

The 110th Tactical Fighter Squadron is based at Lambert Field, St Louis, from where the first of 5079 Phantoms (the prototype F4H-1, 142259) emerged from the nearby McDonnell plant to make its maiden flight on 27 May 1958. The unit operated the F-4C from 1979 until 1984, when it transitioned to the ubiquitous F-4E.

Left After flying the North American F-100 Super Sabre for sixteen years, the 110th TFS received the F-4C during 1979. The F-4C model made its first flight on 27 May 1963; it retained the nose radome shape, folding wings and tailhook of the Navy F-4B, but featured larger tyres and a reconfigured rear-cockpit with full dual flying controls (F-4C 64-749)

Below With the acquisition of the F-4E, the 110th TFS began to apply sharkmouths to its aircraft. The F-4E is equipped with an M61A1 Vulcan six-barrel 20 mm cannon in the nose with provision for 640 rounds. An additional (seventh) fuel cell in the fuselage counter-balances the weight of the weapon (F-4E 68-410; *Mike Kopack*)

Overleaf The Missouri ANG had the honour of hosting the 30th anniversary celebrations of the first flight of the Phantom in May 1988. The aircraft which the 110th TFS chose to decorate for the occasion destroyed two MiG-21s with AIM-9 Sidewinders in SE Asia on 31 May and 16 September 1972 (F-4E 68-338; *Don Spering/AIR*)

MIG-21
31 MAY '72

CAPT. BRUCE G. LEONARD, JR. AC
CAPT. JEFFREY S. FEINSTEIN, WSO

MIG-21
16 SEPT. '72

CAPT. CALVIN B. TIBBET, AC
ILT. WILLIAM S. HARGROVE, WSO

Above The tail markings of 68-338 (the wing commander's aircraft), with the special 30th anniversary logo and a unique representation of the ANG badge, which is under the famous Gateway Arch, a landmark of St Louis

Left Close up of the MiG kill markings applied to the jet intake splitter plate of Phantom 68-338

Texas
111th FIS

Assigned to the air defence role at Ellington Field, south of Houston, the 111th Fighter Interceptor Squadron exchanged its McDonnell F-101B Voodoos for the F-4C during 1981. Late in 1986, the unit transitioned to the F-4D model, which remained on strength until the arrival of the General Dynamics F-16A Fighting Falcon at the end of 1989.

The 111th FIS painted the same distinctive markings on its fleet of F-4Cs as it had previously applied to its Voodoos; the fin flash is a stylized Texan flag (F-4C 64-828; *Douglas E Slowiak/Vortex Photo Graphics*)

Most of the F-4Ds delivered to the 111th FIS were finished in the Europe One camouflage scheme. The fin flash provided a welcome splash of colour, as all other markings were painted black (F-4D 65-676)

Ultimately, all of the unit's F-4Ds were resprayed in the matt Egypt One tactical grey scheme. F-4Ds were widely deployed with the Air Force Reserve and ANG units after being released by the USAF, which received a total of 793 'Deltas' between March 1966 and December 1969 (F-4D 65-721)

Indiana, 113th TFS

The 113th Tactical Fighter Squadron was the last ANG unit to operate the North American F-100 Super Sabre, finally relinquishing its venerable 'Huns' in favour of the F-4C at the end of 1979. The unit is based at Hulman Field, near Terre Haute, hence the HF tailcode. In 1987, the 113th TFS 'traded in' its F-4Cs for a fleet of relatively youthful F-4Es.

Below The F-4Cs were delivered to the 113th TFS wearing standard SE Asia camouflage, but there was no escape from the subsequent application of Europe One. This clean machine bears the marking *Coronet Pawnee-Norway 86* on the vertical stabilizer, evidence of a transatlantic deployment in support of NATO forces (F-4C 63-7437)

Above right The Hulman Field flightline of 1987 reveals the only F-4C in the 113th TFS which was repainted in the latest Egypt One scheme (F-4C 63-7607)

Below right An F-4E of the 113th TFS attending Gunsmoke '89 at Nellis AFB, Nevada. Organized by the USAF Tactical Fighter Weapons Center, Gunsmoke is a biennial Air Force-wide tactical gunnery and bombing competition. The unit's F-4Es mostly came from the 347th Tactical Fighter Wing at Moody AFB, Georgia (F-4E 68-418; *Robert Pfannenschmidt*)

Oregon 114th TFTS

The 114th Tactical Fighter Training Squadron is based at Kingsley Field, near Klamath Falls in southern Oregon. Assigned to the 142nd Fighter Interceptor Group, the unit was first established as the 8123rd Fighter Interceptor Training Squadron on 1 January 1983, tasked with training F-4 crews for the air defence role. The unit was redesignated the 114th TFTS on 1 January 1984, and transitioned from the F-4C to the F-16 Air Defense Fighter during 1988.

Right The F-4Cs of the 114th TFTS were decorated with a particularly attractive eagle marking on the vertical stabilizer. A star attraction at the London International Airshow, Canada in June 1988, this immaculate F-4C features a matching eagle design on the belly fuel tank. When serving with the 8th Tactical Fighter Wing, the 'Wolfpack', at Ubon, Thailand, 64-838 shot down a MiG-21 during Operation Bolo on 2 January 1967 (F-4C 64-838)

Below An F-4C of the 114th TFTS recovers at Kingsley Field in July 1986; unusually, the flight refuelling receptacle, aft of the cockpit, is exposed. Compared to the Navy F-4B, the C-model had completely revised avionics with a Westinghouse APQ-100 radar, Litton type ASN-48 (LN12A/B) inertial navigation system and the aforementioned dorsal refuelling receptacle instead of the Navy's probe (F-4C 63-7482)

Above Sadly, the eagle marking of the 114th TFTS was not immune from the low-visibility virus which spread from the USAF to the ANG, being applied in various shades of grey (F-4C 64-754)

Right Wings of eagles: a box formation of F-4Cs of the 114th TFTS cruise across Crater Lake National Park, near Klamath Falls (*TSgt W R Stine, 114th TFTS*)

District of Columbia, 121st TFS

The 121st Tactical Fighter Squadron has the distinction of being the only ANG unit to have the President of the United States as its Commander-in-Chief in both state and federal capacities. Based at Andrews AFB, Maryland the unit operated the F-4D from 1981 until 1989.

Left Externally virtually identical to previous Phantoms, equipment changes inside the F-4D included the partly solid-state APQ-109 fire-control radar; ASG-22 lead-computing optical sight; an improved ASG-63 INS; and an ASQ-91 weapon release computer, which made the aircraft capable of delivering 'smart' bombs. The red fin cap of these 121st TFS F-4Ds now has four stars; the black DC tailcode is shadowed in white (*Don Spering/AIR*)

Below Wearing Europe One wrap-around camouflage, this aircraft displays the squadron badge on the jet intake, red fin cap with three stars and a fuselage band aft of the cockpit, the latter feature denoting the squadron commander's personal mount (F-4D 66-7693)

Right The handsome gloss black radome of this aircraft was subsequently replaced by a grey one so as to conform with the Egypt One camouflage scheme (F-4D 66-7688; *Regent Dansereau*)

Above Photographed in February 1989, the squadron commander's aircraft not only has special tail markings and a stripe on the jet intakes, but is also waxed to a 'Ray-Bans required' glossy finish. By early 1990, the 121st TFS would be totally re-equipped with the F-16A 'Electric Jet'. Fittingly, this Phantom is now on static display at Andrews AFB (F-4D 66-7693; *Peter Becker*)

Left MiG-killer: taxiing at the Gulfport ANG training site, Mississippi while competing in Fangsmoke '87, 66-7661 displays the artistry of the unit's groundcrews. The white markings were made with chalk, easily washed away back at Andrews. Fangsmoke determines which squadron represents the ANG at the following Gunsmoke tactical bombing and gunnery competition (F-4D 66-7661; *Don Spering/AIR*)

Above An airborne view of MiG-killer 66-7661 repainted in Egypt One camouflage. Captured by the eminent Don Spering as the Phantom was being withdrawn from the 121st TFS in December 1989, this F-4D earned its red star by blowing apart a North Vietnamese MiG-21 on 11 May 1972, while flying with the 555th TFS (F-4D 66-7661; *Don Spering/AIR*)

Louisiana, 122nd TFS

Based at Naval Air Station New Orleans, the 122nd Tactical Fighter Squadron operated the F-4C from 1979 until 1986, when it became the first ANG unit to receive the McDonnell Douglas F-15A Eagle air superiority fighter.

Right Painted in classic SE Asia camouflage, this Phantom is parked next to a Super Sabre—the type it replaced in the 122nd TFS. A discrete *LOUISIANA* motif is rendered on top of the vertical stabilizer (F-4C 63-7506; *Daniel Soulaine Collection*)

Below The Gulf of Mexico, February 1982: at this stage in the Phantom's career with the 122nd TFS, the tail markings had been toned down from white to black (F-4C 63-7522; *Don Spering/AIR*)

Overleaf The 122nd TFS operated six of their F-4s in a temporary blue-grey camouflage scheme during 1983. For a short period, the unit also applied its nickname, *Coonass Militia*, on the vertical stabilizer of most of its aircraft (F-4C 63-7637; *Daniel Soulaine Collection*)

Oregon, 123rd FIS

After converting from the McDonnell F-101B Voodoo, the 123rd Fighter Interceptor Squadron operated the F-4C from 1982 until 1989, when the unit took delivery of F-15A/B Eagles released by the disbandment of the 318th FIS, USAF at McChord AFB, Washington State. Based at Portland International Airport, the 123rd FIS also maintained a detachment of F-4Cs on alert status at nearby Kingsley Field.

Taxiing at Tyndall AFB, Florida after a live-firing sortie during the William Tell '84 weapons meet, this Phantom had its Sidewinder AAM safetied as soon as it cleared the runway. The F-4C could accept a total of four AIM-9 Sidewinder infrared-guided missiles on the two inboard wing pylons, and four AIM-7 Sparrow semi-active radar-homing missiles carried semi-submerged in well mountings under the fuselage (F-4C 64-713)

The 123rd FIS flight-line in August 1986; this F-4 has a funnel attached to the wing fuel vent as the summer heat makes jetfuel expand and overflow (F-4C 64-852)

Egypt One camouflage in all its dullness: the aircraft is painted in two tones of grey, and the diving eagle on the tail is plain grey (F-4C 64-713)

Photographed in May 1986, this Phantom displays an early version of the low-visibility grey camouflage scheme. The aircraft is painted in three tones of grey, rather than the two adopted subsequently; the tail marking is outlined in dark grey only. A triple MiG-killer during the Vietnam War, 66-776 destroyed one MiG-21 on 23 April 1967, and two MiG-21s on 22 May 1967 (F-4C 64-776; *Patrick Martin*)

Kansas, 127th TFS and 177th TFTS

The 127th Tactical Fighter Squadron transitioned from the Republic F-105D Thunderchief to the F-4D in August 1979. Shortly thereafter, the 177th Tactical Fighter Training Squadron was created, and associated with the 127th TFS in order to train ANG crews on the Phantom. Controlled by the 184th Tactical Fighter Group, the two squadrons shared a pool of F-4Ds at McConnell AFB.

Left 'Zapped' on the jet intake at Canadian Forces Base Bagotville in August 1983, this Phantom also displays the *JAYHAWKS* nickname of the 127th TFS on its travel pod (F-4D 65-759)

Below During its eleven-year association with the Phantom, the 184th TFG operated no less than 65 F-4Ds and trained more than 1200 aircrews. A few of the group's aircraft were painted in the grey of Air Defense Command, highlighted by the 184th TFG badge in full colour (F-4D 65-749; *Don Spering/AIR*)

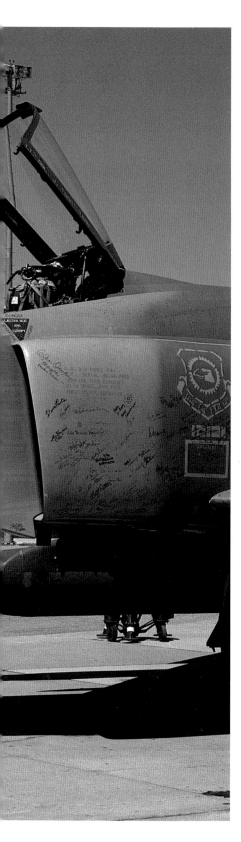

Above A double MiG-killer, 66-0271 blasted two North Vietnamese MiG-21s out of the sky on 18/29 July 1972. This Phantom is now a gate guardian at McConnell AFB, where it was dedicated with due ceremony on 31 March 1990—the last day of F-4 operations with the 184th TFG (F-4D 66-0271; *Douglas E Slowiak/Vortex Photo Graphics*)

Left On 31 March 1990, when the final eight Phantoms from the 184th TFG departed for the Aerospace Maintenance And Recovery Center at Davis - Monthan AFB in Arizona, 66-7553 fell victim to hydraulic failure and had to return to McConnell AFB. Pending its repair, the aircraft was decorated with signatures and graffiti (F-4D 66-7553)

Above Right up to the end, the F-4s of the Kansas ANG were fully mission-capable. Intense concentration is required during a low-level sortie, terrain-avoidance being priority number one (F-4D 65-782; *Don Spering/AIR*)

Left Old fighters never die, they simply fly to Davis-Monthan. En route to the 'boneyard' on 31 March 1990, the pilot of this Phantom prepares to 'fill 'er up' for the last time using a KC-135 tanker. The Phantom's refuelling receptacle, aft of the cockpit, is ready and waiting for the nozzle of the flying boom (F-4D 66-7768; *Don Spering/AIR*)

Georgia, 128th TFS

Based at Dobbins AFB, the 128th Tactical Fighter Squadron has the distinction of being the ANG unit which operated the Phantom for the shortest period of time, from early 1983 until 1986. By the end of 1986, the 128th TFS had become the second ANG squadron to convert to the F-15 Eagle.

Not Georgia, but Soesterberg AB in The Netherlands, where the 128th TFS deployed in August 1985. Several ANG units fly across 'The Pond' every year, giving aircrews invaluable experience of European weather and the NATO operational environment (F-4D 66-7714; *Ruud van Nimwegen*)

Vermont, 134th TFS

The 134th Tactical Fighter Squadron took delivery of their F-4Ds in 1981, having operated the Martin EB-57 as a Defense Systems Evaluation Squadron since 1974. Nicknamed The Green Mountain Boys, the unit is based at Burlington International Airport.

Below A mixed-up F-4D photographed in May 1982, with upside down national insignia and the unit's distinctive yellow band missing from the tail. However, all is not lost as *The Green Mountain Boys* nickname is just visible (F-4D 66-7457)

Right In the twilight of its service with the 134th TFS, an F-4D receives attention on the flight-line at Burlington. In 1986, the unit transitioned to the F-16A, initially retaining its TFS designation. However, in 1988 the primary role of The Green Mountain Boys was changed, and the unit reverted to their original designation as the 134th Fighter Interceptor Squadron (F-4D 65-730; *Regent Dansereau*)

New York, 136th FIS

Based at Niagara Falls International Airport, the 136th Fighter Interceptor Squadron operated the F-4C from the beginning of 1982 until this model was replaced by the F-4D in 1987. In common with many other ANG units, the 136th FIS became an enthusiastic convert to the F-16 during the summer of 1990.

Left An immaculate two-ship formation of F-4Cs, each of which has a different presentation of the serial number on the tail; the location of the ANG badge on the leading aircraft is noteworthy. The F-4C was powered by two General Electric J79-GE-15 turbojets with a sea-level thrust rating of 17,000 lb with afterburning

Below In their early days with the 136th FIS, the F-4Ds lacked the rainbow rudder markings and were identified by a simple *Niagara Falls* motif on top of the vertical stabilizer (F-4D 66-7491)

Above The rhino marking is known to have been applied to the following F-4Ds: 65-677, 65-792, 66-0259, 66-7456, 66-7485 and 66-7491

Below left For the William Tell '88 weapons meet, the 136th FIS added a rhino marking to its participating Phantoms. This aircraft, noted at McConnell AFB, Kansas in mid-1989, evidently retained its horny friend (F-4D 66-7456)

Above left As late as June 1988, this Phantom still retained the attractive overall light gloss grey air defence scheme (F- 4D 65-692)

New Jersey, 141st TFS

The 141st Tactical Fighter Squadron were mounted on the Republic F-105B Thunderchief for 18 years before transitioning to the F-4D in 1981. Based at McGuire AFB, the unit converted to the F-4E in 1985.

Right On a hot July afternoon, a member of the groundcrew shelters from the sun in the shadow of a SE Asia camouflaged F-4D (F-4D 65-644)

Below An Egypt One camouflaged F-4E receives attention on the McGuire flight-line. The open nose radome reveals the Westinghouse AN/APQ-120 fire-control radar pulled out from its compartment; the antenna dish has been removed (F-4E 68-526; *Regent Dansereau*)

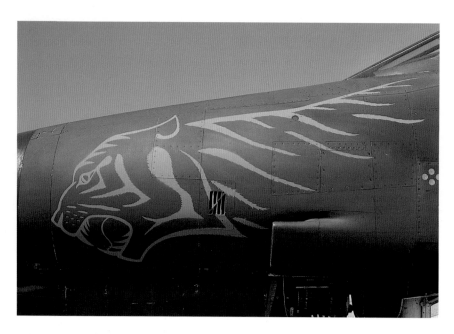

Above An early 'low visibility' tiger marking painted in tan over a European One camouflaged F-4E (*Regent Dansereau*)

Right The mascot of the 141st TFS is the Bengal Tiger, the head of which is represented on the nose of this Europe One camouflaged F-4E. Sadly, it has proved impractical for the unit to fly an aircraft all the way to Europe for the annual NATO Tiger Meets (F-4E 68-527)

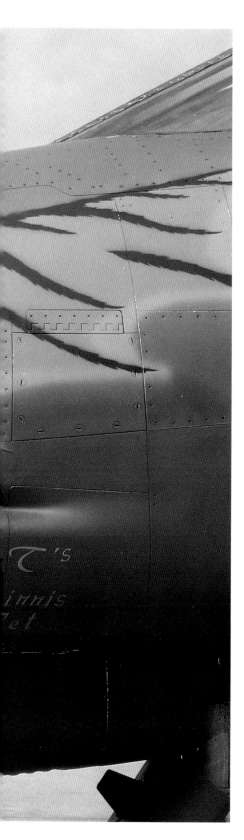

Above From 1989, the tiger markings on the Europe One camouflage F- 4Es were decorated in their proper colours—an impressive improvement (F-4E 68-392)

Left The ferocious feline in close-up; the colours are well suited to emerge from the Europe One 'forest' camouflage. The Phantom 'Spook' is visible on the small air intake (F-4E 68-392)

Above A much less attractive version of the tiger's head on the nose of this taxiing Egypt One camouflaged F-4E. The 141st TFS is scheduled to re-equip with F-16 Fighting Falcons in 1992 (F-4E 68-401)

Right Displaying an interesting variation of camouflage schemes and squadron markings, these F-4Es were photographed in May 1988 (*Don Spering/AIR*)

Above Most of the F-4Es supplied to the 141st TFS were previously operated by the 86th Tactical Fighter Wing, based at Ramstein AB in Germany. When they came on strength, the aircraft acquired the same unit markings as applied to the F-4Ds (*Don Spering/AIR*)

Right An impressive line-up of thirteen F-4Ds at McGuire AFB in August 1985; three aircraft have yet to be repainted in Europe One, substituting the tan colour for dark grey (*Don Spering/AIR*)

Mississippi, 153rd TRS

The 153rd Tactical Reconnaissance Squadron is based at Key Field, near Meridian, where the unit was activated in 1939. Dedicated to the reconnaissance role since 1952, the unit received the RF-4C in 1978, having successfully operated the RF-51D Mustang, RF-80 Shooting Star, RF-84F Thunderflash and RF-101C Voodoo.

Below Packed with sophisticated reconnaissance sensors and communications systems, the re-shaped nose of the RF-4C is equipped with forward, oblique, lateral and panoramic cameras; a large sideways-looking airborne radar (SLAR); and infrared linescan. This wrap-around camouflaged recce-bird displays the KE tailcode and a black scallop with *Mississippi*, the ANG badge, and the outline in gold (RF-4C 66-423)

Above right The introduction of the Egypt One paint scheme resulted in the squadron markings being simplified. Gone is the ANG badge and black scallop, but gold paint is still used for the squadron badge on the fuselage and to shadow the stylized *MISSISSIPPI* and the serial number. The exhaust area on this aircraft is highly polished (RF-4C 66-413)

Below right A magnolia flower, and black and gold markings were applied to this pristine machine in 1989 to commemorate the 50th anniversary of the Mississippi ANG (RF-4C 66-430; *Tom Hildreth*)

Alabama, 160th TRS/TFS

The 160th Tactical Reconnaissance Squadron received the RF-4C in mid-1971. Based at Dannely Field, near Montgomery, the unit was redesignated the 160th Tactical Fighter Squadron when it transitioned to the F-4D during 1983. The F-16 joined the ranks of the 160th TFS in 1989.

The prototype RF-4C made its first flight on 18 May 1964. Photographed a decade later, this well-worn recce-Phantom displays the old-style ANG badge on the tail. The squadron badge is carried aft of the jet intake, while the *ALABAMA* motif is borne on top of the vertical stabilizer (RF-4C 64-997; *Daniel Soulaine Collection*)

Six years later in 1980, the same Phantom is captured during a deployment to Germany. Special markings were applied to the rudder for the occasion; note *Montgomery* in gold on the red tail band (RF-4C 64-997; *Daniel Soulaine Collection*)

Above A pair of RF-4Cs of the 160th TRS cruise above the clouds, the summer 1981 date indicated by wrap-around camouflage and black tailcodes. The radar in the nose is a compact APQ-99 set for mapping and terrain-avoidance (*Don Spering/AIR*)

Right The 160th TFS deployed several F-4Ds to Soesterberg AB in The Netherlands in the summer of 1985. Having transitioned to the F-4D, the unit adopted the AL tailcode. The black anti-glare panel is of extended area and has a red and white border (F-4D 66-7754; *Ruud van Nimwegen*)

Indiana, 163rd TFS

The 163rd Tactical Fighter Squadron converted from the F-100D Super Sabre to the F-4C in 1979. Based at Fort Wayne Municipal Airport, the unit transitioned to the F-4E during 1986.

Left An F-4C painted in SE Asia camouflage, consisting of two tones of green and tan over a light grey underside. Note the Outstanding Unit Award ribbon applied forward of the ANG badge (F-4C 63-7513; *Jim Nugent*)

Below Technicians toil in the engine bay of this F-4C parked on the ANG ramp at Fort Wayne Municipal Airport in 1982. A 370 US gal wing fuel tank is supported on its transportation dolly in front of the aircraft (F-4C 63-7474; *Duncan MacIntosh via Bryan Beaton*)

In common with the New Jersey ANG, most of the F-4Es received by the 163rd TFS were transferred from the 86th TFW at Ramstein AB in Germany. This wrap-around camouflaged Phantom displays the same squadron markings as applied to the preceding F-4Cs. Under the cockpit are the names of the pilot and his weapon systems officer (WSO), although they would rarely fly their assigned aircraft (F-4E 68-517; *Douglas E Slowiak/Vortex Photo Graphics*)

The wing commander's individually marked F-4E holds for 'last chance' external checks before launching from McConnell AFB, Kansas in April 1990. The 163rd TFS is controlled by the 122nd TFW (F-4E 68-444)

Kentucky, 165th TRS

Based at Louisville Municipal Airport, the 165th Tactical Reconnaissance Squadron maintained its assigned role for 30 years, having been successively equipped with the Martin RB-57B, McDonnell RF-101G/H Voodoo and RF-4C Phantom II. A complete change of mission occurred in 1989, when the unit became a Tactical Airlift Squadron after converting to the Lockheed C-130 Hercules.

When the 165th TRS deployed to Denmark in 1982, the rudder of each Phantom was decorated with 'Old Glory' superimposed by an eagle. The jet intake carries the flags of Denmark, NATO and the USA, as well as *Best Focus '82*, the codename of the exercise (RF-4C 64-1084; *Daniel Soulaine Collection*)

The unit was never at a loss when it came to applying special tail markings for various deployments and exercises. This aircraft features a large pegasus on the tail, together with *PHANTOMS FINEST* in red, white and blue (RF-4C 65-885; *Robert Conely*)

Above The 14,410 ft peak of Mount Rainier is clearly visible behind this RF-4C of the 165th TRS on the ramp at McChord AFB, Washington State in July 1988. Most of the low-visibility grey RF-4Cs carried the *PHANTOMS FINEST* marking (RF-4C 65-873; *Patrick Martin*)

Left Not long after this shot was taken at the end of 1988, the 165th TRS swapped their fast jets for C-130 'Fat Alberts', having operated the RF-4C since 1976. These aircraft display a slight variation in the low-visibility paint scheme. Many of the ex-165th TRS Phantoms went to the 190th TRS, Idaho ANG but 65-822 is one of eight RF-4Cs transferred to the Spanish Air Force (*Don Spering/AIR*)

Illinois, 170th TFS

Based at Capital International Airport, near Springfield, the 170th Tactical Fighter Squadron was the first ANG unit to receive the F-4C, having transitioned from the Republic F-84F Thunderstreak in January 1972. F-4Ds arrived in January 1981, and served until earning honourable retirement in October 1989, when the unit officially transitioned to the F-16A.

Left Photographed in 1974, this F-4C wears standard SE Asia camouflage and has the old ANG badge on the tail (F-4C 64-822; *Douglas E Slowiak/Vortex Photo Graphics*)

Below As the 170th TFS transitioned to the F-4C, six RF-4Cs were borrowed for proficiency training. Despite their temporary assignment, these recce-Phantoms received full squadron markings, including the unit badge on the jet intake (RF-4C 65-875; *Ben Knowles Jr via Patrick Martin*)

Right In July 1980, this F-4C still retains SE Asia camouflage paint, but is now adorned with the newer ANG badge. The squadron badge is carried on the starboard side of the aircraft , the group badge of the 183rd TFG to port. Tail band colours varied from one aircraft to another (F-4C 64-0691; *Douglas E Slowiak/Vortex Photo Graphics*)

Above When the F-4Ds were repainted in the Egypt One camouflage scheme, the size of the tailcode and serial number was temporarily reduced. The SI tailcode (for Springfield, Illinois), was added in 1984 (F-4D 66-7659)

Michigan, 171st FIS

The 171st Fighter Interceptor Squadron was the first ANG unit to transition from the Convair F-106 Delta Dart to the Phantom, their F-4Cs arriving at Selfridge ANGB in 1978. From 1986 until the arrival of the F-16 Air Defense Fighter in 1990, the unit operated the F-4D.

The Phantoms of the 171st FIS were famous for their unmistakeable black and yellow checkerboards and nose art. True professionals in their checkerboard helmets, this crew prepare to 'split the apple' at the 1984 William Tell weapons meet (F-4C 63-7475)

Above *Shadow Demon* painted on F-4C 63-7514 (*Bryan Beaton*)

Above right *Don't mess with the kid*, with Bugs Bunny character, was applied to F-4C 64-707 (*Bryan Beaton*)

Left Most of the F-4Ds supplied to the 171st FIS had the Europe One scheme, but were gradually repainted in either Egypt One (as here), or the by now uncommon gloss grey finish with full squadron markings. Pictured in July 1987, the checkerboards and stylized *Michigan* on this aircraft are subdued to blend in with the low-visibility camouflage (F-4D 65-668; *Mike Kopack*)

Above Gunfighter! Although only three are visible, no less than five SUU-23A 20 mm gunpods were fitted to this Phantom for an airshow at Selfridge in July 1988. A single gunpod on the centreline (station 5) was quite adequate for strafing missions; the time to maximum firing rate (6000 rounds per minute) is 0.3 seconds. The F-4D could carry virtually every type of weapon in the USAF inventory (F-4D 66-0243; *Bryan Beaton*)

Right In 'dirty' configuration with landing gear, flaps and leading edge devices deployed, a pair of F-4Cs recover to Selfridge ANGB (*Don Spering/AIR*)

Nebraska, 173rd TRS

The 173rd Tactical Reconnaissance Squadron acquired its RF-4Cs in 1972, ending a happy association with the veteran Republic RF-84F Thunderstreak. The unit continues to operate its recce-Phantoms from Lincoln Municipal Airport.

Left Not a previously unknown camouflage scheme, merely the effect of preparing the aircraft's skin before the application of low-visibility greys (RF-4C 64-1039; *Craig Baldwin*)

Below The commanding officer's RF-4C, with the red, yellow and blue colours of each flight in the squadron on the fincap, superimposed by *Huskers*, the nickname of the 173rd TRS. The location of the serial number is unusual (RF-4C 64-1066; *Douglas E Slowiak/Vortex Photo Graphics*)

North Dakota, 178th FIS

Dedicated to the air defence role since the era of the Lockheed F-94 Starfire in the fifties, the 178th Fighter Interceptor Squadron was, in 1977, the first ANG unit to receive the F-4D. Based at Hector Field (Fargo Municipal Airport), the squadron transitioned to the F-16 Air Defense Fighter at the end of 1989.

Below Most of the F-4Ds supplied to the 178th TFS came from the USAF 49th TFW at Holloman AFB, New Mexico, being operated in SE Asia camouflage until repainted in the air defence grey scheme. The ANG badge was carried on the jet intake, and the last two digits of the serial were enlarged (F-4D 64- 975; *Douglas E Slowiak/Vortex Photo Graphics*)

Above right The victim of a fine piece of 'zapping' in April 1981 by personnel unknown of the Canadian Armed Forces, this F-4D displays a unique variation of the US 'star and bar', complete with maple leaf, on the fuselage (F-4D 64-973; *Douglas E Slowiak/Vortex Photo Graphics*)

Below right Riding the combined 34,000-lb of afterburning thrust produced by its J79-GE-15 turbojets, a Phantom departs Hector Field; the pilot has obviously wasted no time in selecting landing gears UP (F-4D 64-970)

Above During 1986, the 178th FIS received some ex-New Jersey ANG Phantoms painted in Europe One; *THE Happy Hooligans* marking was soon applied. This aircraft has evidently 'borrowed' a grey fuel tank (F-4D 66-7498; *Craig Baldwin*)

Left A low-visibility Phantom attending the Maple Leaf '89 air defence exercise, hosted by the Vermont ANG (F-4D 64-968)

Above The 178th FIS repainted this aircraft to commemorate the centennial of the state of North Dakota, and it retained its superb colour scheme for several months in 1989 before reverting to low-visibility grey (F-4D 66-7498; *Harold Homuth*)

Opposite The 'Blue Jet' featured an impressive painting on its undersurface; the design represents the state flag of North Dakota (F-4D 66-7498; *Major Larry L Harrington, North Dakota ANG*)

Right The large fuselage marking, representing the family of a pioneer, was the official state centennial logo (F-4D 66-7498; *Douglas E Slowiak/Vortex Photo Graphics*)

Minnesota, 179th TRS/ TFS

In 1976, the Minnesota ANG relinquished its McDonnell F-101B Voodoo interceptors for the RF-4C recce-version of the Phantom II, being designated as the 179th Tactical Reconnaissance Squadron. However, seven years later, the unit was redesignated as the 179th Tactical Fighter Squadron when the F-4D replaced its RF-4Cs. The 179th TFS transitioned to the F-16A in 1990.

Below A Vietnam veteran, this recce-Phantom has the standard SE Asia camouflage scheme with white stencilings. At first sight not easy to distinguish from the fighter models, the RF-4C was unarmed except for a capability to carry a tactical nuclear bomb on the centreline (RF-4C 64-1061; *Alberto Storti*)

Right A new tail marking, consisting of stars representing the Big Dipper constellation, was adopted when the squadron received its F-4Ds in late 1983. This Phantom shot down a North Vietnamese MiG-21 on 12 September 1972 (F-4D 65-608; *Daniel Soulaine Collection*)

The 179th TFS flirted with this squadron marking in the mid-eighties, but it was not adopted. The unusual size of the serial number and the location of the ANG badge is noteworthy (F-4D 65-586; *Minnesota ANG via Patrick Martin*)

A Phantom receives a 'last chance' inspection before take-off; groundcrews check for hydraulic or fuel leaks and also remove the remaining safety pins on the landing gears and weapon stations. Squadron markings were toned down so as to conform with the low-visibility grey camouflage (F-4D 64-930)

Texas, 182nd TFS

Based at Kelly AFB near San Antonio, the 182nd Tactical Fighter Squadron transitioned from the F-100D Super Sabre to the F-4C in 1979. In 1986, the Texans became the second ANG unit to convert to the F-16A Fighting Falcon.

Displaying the same squadron markings as applied to the preceding Super Sabres, this Phantom retains its SE Asia camouflage (F-4C 63-7449; *Daniel Soulaine Collection*)

Left On patrol high above the 'Lone Star' state, a pair of F-4Cs display a slight variation in the SE Asia camouflage scheme. Very few pilots actually did it, but if full afterburner was selected most Phantoms were capable of Mach 2 at altitude (*Don Spering/AIR*)

Above Several Phantoms were oversprayed with a temporary coat of light grey paint for the Red Flag '84 exercise at Nellis AFB, Nevada. Few of the original markings remain visible, but the SA (for San Antonio) tailcode is still discernible. This camouflage trial was a foretaste of the dull low-visibility paint scheme (F-4C 63-7585; *Kirk Minert via Marty Isham*)

Arkansas, 184th TFS

Based at Fort Smith Municipal Airport, the 184th Tactical Fighter Squadron operated the F-4C from 1979 until 1988, when the unit transitioned to the F-16A Fighting Falcon.

A truly cost-effective purchase by 'Uncle Sam', this old warrior of the 184th TFS has relatively simple unit markings: a red tail and canopy stripes, and a razorback in a lozenge on the jet intake (F-4C 64-919; *Douglas E Slowiak/Vortex Photo Graphics*)

Idaho, 189th TRTF/190th TRS

Formerly mounted on the Convair F-102 Delta Dagger interceptor, the 190th Tactical Reconnaissance Squadron received its RF-4Cs in 1975. The 189th Tactical Reconnaissance Training Flight was subsequently established to complement the 190th TFS and provide recce-crews for all ANG RF-4C squadrons. Both units are based at Boise Municipal Airport.

Right The discrete unit marking was slightly modified in 1986, when a small white cap appeared on the '*A*' of *IDAHO*, and stylized mountains were added (RF-4C 65-849; *Keith Snyder*)

Below The Idaho ANG is currently operating most of the twenty block 40 RF-4Cs equipped with AN/ARN-92 LORAN (LOng RAnge Navigation) gear developed for Vietnam operations; the aircraft have a distinctive 'towel rack' antenna on the dorsal spine (RF-4C 68-606)

Nevada, 192nd TRS

Based at Reno Municipal Airport, the Nevada ANG operated the Martin RB- 57B and recce-versions of the McDonnell F-101 Voodoo before it received the RF-4C in 1975. The High Rollers nickname of the 192nd Tactical Reconnaissance Squadron has perhaps been influenced by the nearby gambling centres of Reno and Las Vegas.

Above right On course for Reno IAP in August 1988, a two-ship of 'grey ghosts' prepare to recover to base as the sun sinks rapidly in the west. The 192nd TRS is integrated into the USAF structure through the 152nd TRG which, if mobilized, would report to Air Combat Command (*Paul F Crickmore*)

Below How low can you go? With the 192nd TRS, obviously very low indeed! Streaking across the desert floor, this aircraft displays the nickname *High Rollers* at the top of the vertical stabilizer and NEVADA in small lettering above the ANG badge (RF-4C 64-029; *Paul F Crickmore*)

Right The 192nd TRS applied this special marking to three of its aircraft for the 1988 Reconnaissance Air Meet (RAM), in which units from the ANG, USAF, PACAF, USN, USMC, *Luftwaffe* and Royal Australian Air Force competed to 'get the pictures' (RF-4C 64-1021; *Keith Snyder*)

California, 194th FIS

The F-4D was the fifth type of jet fighter to be assigned to the 194th Fighter Interceptor Squadron since it began operating F-86A Sabres in October 1954. The squadron converted to F-86Ls in 1958, to F-102A Delta Daggers in 1964, F-106A Delta Darts in 1974, and to F-4Ds in 1984. Based at Fresno Air Terminal, the 194th FIS transitioned to the F-16 Air Defense Fighter in 1989.

Above right Early in 1988, the 194th FIS changed the tail marking of its F-4s, adopting the griffin motif from the squadron badge. The insignia of Tactical Air Command appeared in the same location on the left side of the vertical stabilizer (F-4D 65-779; *Daniel Soulaine Collection*)

Below right Fresno, April 1988: this Phantom is finished in the definitive camouflage and markings used by the 194th FIS until the unit transitioned to the F-16 a year later (F-4D 65-646; *Patrick Martin*)

Below Still finished in Vietnam-era wrap-around camouflage, this aircraft is fitted with a pair of light gloss grey 370-US gal wing tanks (F-4D 65-646; *Douglas E Slowiak/Vortex Photo Graphics*)

In 1986, aircraft and crews from the 194th FIS joined those from the North Dakota and Minnesota ANG units which deployed to Ramstein, Germany in an operation codenamed *Creek Klaxon*. As detachment 11, these assets took over the alert duty from the 86th TFW while this USAFE unit converted from F-4Es to F-16Cs (F-4D 65-0747; *René J Francillon*)

California, 196th TFS/TRS

After operating the Cessna O-2A 'push-pull' piston-twin in the forward air control (FAC) role since 1975, the unit re-equipped with the F-4C as the 196th Tactical Fighter Squadron in 1983. The arrival of noisy fast jets necessitated a move from Ontario International Airport to March AFB. The 196th TFS converted to F-4Es in the spring of 1987, most of their C-models going to museums. Although scheduled to receive the Rockwell OA-10 Bronco turboprop FAC aircraft, the unit managed to retain its association with the Phantom by re-equipping with RF-4Cs in 1990, thereby being redesignated as the 196th Tactical Reconnaissance Squadron.

Left Egypt One, Europe One: during the transition phase, the 196th TFS operated the F-4E and F-4C together in the spring of 1987. The built-in M61A1 cannon installation of the F-4E required a nose 57 inches longer; E-models also have leading edge manoeuvre slats (*René J Francillon*)

Below The star-studded markings applied to the F-4Cs were similar to those carried by the F-102 Delta Daggers which, as the 163rd Fighter Interceptor Squadron, the unit flew before the best-forgotten O-2 era began in the mid-seventies (F-4C 63-7426; *René J Francillon*)

Above The RF-4Cs of the 196th TRS are the oldest Phantoms in service anywhere in the world, being amongst the initial batch delivered to the USAF in 1964–65. The squadron markings are virtually the same as those applied to the preceding F-4Es of the 196th TFS (RF-4C 64-1053; *Bob Niedermeier*)

Right A few F-4Cs were repainted in the Egypt One paint scheme before the squadron transitioned to the F-4E. Awaiting take-off clearance, this aircraft is armed with a single AIM-9 Sidewinder and has a 600-US gal ventral fuel tank. Note the small size of the serial number (F-4C 64-682; *René J Francillon*)

Hawaii, 199th TFS

Based at Hickam AFB, the 199th Tactical Fighter Squadron operated the F-4C from 1976 until mid 1987, when it transitioned to the F-15A Eagle. Assigned to the Pacific Air Forces (PACAF), the primary mission of the unit is the air defence of the Hawaiian Islands.

The Hawaii ANG flew the F-102 Delta Dagger interceptor for fifteen years before converting to the F-4C in October 1976. The new tail-band adopted for the Phantom represents the nine Hawaiian channels (lower row); the six yellow arrows on the middle row symbolize the warriors from the six major populated islands; and the top row shows the five major mountains of the Hawaiian Islands with clouds in between (F-4C 63-7540)

On the ramp at Hickam, the groundcrew wait for the pilot and GIB ('guy in back') to sort themselves out before commencing the engine start sequence (F-4C 64-913)

Noted in November 1984 at Hickam AFB, 63-7632 was one of the first
recipients of this highly effective camouflage finish. Known variously as Egypt
One, Hill Grey or low-visibility grey, the scheme was, to the dismay of many
enthusiasts, widely adopted (F-4C 63-7632)